Garfield Holiday Celebrations

(Originally published as *Garfield's Jolly Holiday 3-Pack*)

JIM DAVIS

Ballantine Books • **New York**

Garfield
in Disguise

JIM DAVIS

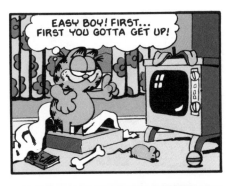

THAT'S A NIGHT WHEN DOGS HAVE TO HELP CATS GO OUT AND GET CANDY

AND IF DOG DOES A GOOD JOB, HE GETS A PIECE OF CANDY OF HIS VERRRY OWN!

WELL DO YOU WANNA GO, BOY? HUH? HUH? WANNA GO OUT AND GET CANDY, HUH? HUH? BOY? WANNA GO? HUH? HUH?

OKAY! LET'S GO TO THE ATTIC AND FIND SOME COSTUMES FOR TONIGHT!

JUST BETWEEN YOU AND ME, THERE'RE TIMES I LOVE THAT DOG

THERE SHOULD BE SOME GREAT HALLOWEEN COSTUMES UP HERE SOMEWHERE, ODIE. JON HAS NEVER THROWN ANYTHING AWAY

I COULD BE AN ASTRONAUT, A ROBOT, A HOBO, A CLOWN...

OR AN ALIEN CREATURE GOING OUT ON THE TOWN

I THINK I HAVE JUST THE COSTUMES FOR US, ODIE

CHOMP, CHOMP, CHOMP

ARRRRR! IT DO BE A LANDLUBBER WHO BE SHOVIN' LASAGNA IN HIS FACE

GIMME!!

OH, HOW CUTE! HERE YOU GO, KIDS

ME THINKS YER BE A MIGHT STINGY WITH YER CANDY, MISS. IF YER DON'T RECONSIDER YOUR CONTRIBUTION I'LL GIVE YER LIVING ROOM DRAPES A TASTE OF ME BROADSWORD

THANK YOU. A THOUSAND BLESSIN'S UPON YER HOME, MA'AM

ARRRRRR! WHAT HAVE WE HERE? WHY IT DO BE A PIRATE SHIP FOR TO TAKE US ACROSS THE RIVER

I COMMANDEER THIS SHIP IN THE NAME OF ORANGE BEARD, THE PIRATE. FREE THE MOORIN'S AND SHOVE OFF MATEY!!

WHAT I AM ABOUT TO TELL YOU HAS NEVER BEEN TOLD TO ANOTHER LIVING SOUL

KABOOM

THIS ISLAND HAS A SECRET... A DEEP, DARK SECRET IT HAS HELD FOR A HUNDRED YEARS. ONE HUNDRED YEARS AGO TONIGHT, A RUTHLESS BAND OF PIRATES HELD UP IN THIS VERY HOUSE. THEY HAD LOOTED MANY SHIPS AND WERE PURSUED BY GOVERNMENT TROOPS

THEY WERE HEAVILY LADEN WITH THEIR ILL-GOTTEN GAINS. THEY HAD TO BURY THE TREASURE BEFORE MAKING THEIR ESCAPE. HOWEVER, BEFORE THEY LEFT THIS ISLAND ON THAT STORMY NIGHT, THEY SIGNED A CONTRACT WRITTEN IN BLOOD...

THEY VOWED TO RETURN FOR THE TREASURE 100 YEARS FROM HALLOWEEN NIGHT... AT THE STROKE OF MIDNIGHT... EVEN IF IT MEANT RETURNING FROM THE GRAVE

KA-BOOM!

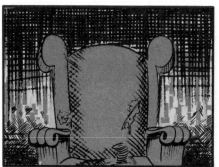

JON IS NEVER GOING TO BELIEVE WHAT HAPPENED TO US TONIGHT. HE PROBABLY THINKS WE WERE OUT SINGING ON THE FENCE AGAIN. WAIT TILL HE SEES ALL THIS CANDY

HAVE WE GOT A SURPRISE FOR HIM!

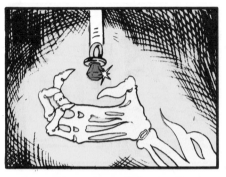

Garfield's
Thanksgiving

JIM DAVIS

GOOD MORNING, JON

SORRY TO DISTURB YOU. I KNOW YOU HAVE A BUSY SOCIAL CALENDAR

BUT IF YOU WILL BE SO KIND AS TO GO TO THE KITCHEN AND FIX ME A HUGE BREAKFAST...

I WILL ALLOW YOU TO COME BACK TO BED TO FINISH YOUR SLEEP

I WASN'T ABOUT TO GIVE HIM THE SATISFACTION OF WAKING ME UP

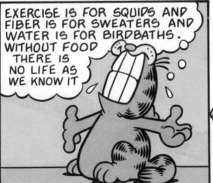

SHOO-BOP-DOO-WOP. GOT A DATE WITH MY DREAM CHICK. GONNA IMPRESS HER AND MAKE HER MY GIRL

OH, WOE IS ME. I'M BEING PUT ON A DIET AND I'M GOING TO DIE

HERE, GARFIELD. HAVE SOME FOOD

ACCORDING TO YOUR DIET, YOU GET THIS

BEDTIME, GARFIELD. WE HAVE TO GET A GOOD NIGHT'S SLEEP BEFORE THE BIG DAY TOMORROW

I MAY NEVER SEE TOMORROW, JON. BE A GOOD FRIEND AND CARRY ME TO BED

YOU'RE A REAL WIMP, GARFIELD. YOU'VE BEEN ON THIS DIET ONLY HALF A DAY

...AND YOU ACT AS THOUGH YOU'VE BEEN STARVING FOR WEEKS

HOURS, WEEKS, WHAT'S THE DIFFERENCE? I'VE ALREADY FORGOTTEN WHAT PIZZA TASTES LIKE

GOOD MORNING, GARFIELD. SLEEP WELL?

WELL, LET'S SEE. WHAT CAN YOU HAVE FOR BREAKFAST THIS MORNING THAT WOULD BE WITHIN YOUR DIET?

A BOWL OF DIRTY DISHWATER WOULD PROBABLY DO THE TRICK. THEN FOR DESSERT, PERHAPS I COULD LICK YOUR SHOES

FOR ME? OH GOSH, JON

ADD WATER, AND DONE!

TO HEAR MOM AND GRANDMA TALK I ALWAYS THOUGHT PREPARING A THANKSGIVING MEAL WAS TOUGH. HA!

OH MY GOSH. I FORGOT TO CALL MOM

THANKSGIVING! HUMBUG! WHAT GOOD IS IT IF YOU'RE ON A DIET? LIFE'S NOT FAIR

SO, IF I CAN'T ENJOY THIS MEAL TODAY, NOBODY WILL!

THAT'S DETERGENT, AND IT TASTES YUCKY. I'M GOING TO MAKE A NICE WHITE SAUCE FOR JON'S VEGETABLES

TAKE THAT, JON. TAKE THAT, THANKSGIVING

SQUIRT SQUIRT SQUIRT

BYE, MOM

NOW FOR MY FAVORITE PART OF THANKSGIVING

DESSERT

GIVE IT YOUR BEST SHOT, JON. IF YOU DON'T RUIN IT, I'LL HELP

HERE IT IS... PUMPKIN PIE

DESSERT DESSERT

"CANNED PUMPKIN", GOT IT, "SUGAR", GOT IT, "SALT", GOT IT, "CINNAMON", GOT IT

"BLEND, POUR INTO SHELL AND BAKE AT 400° FOR 50 MINUTES"

EASY AS PIE. HA,HA. GET IT? PIE?

PIE, GOT IT

I'D BETTER SPRUCE MYSELF UP A BIT

SO, GARFIELD, HOW'S YOUR DIET? I SEE YOU'RE STILL THE SIZE OF AN AIRCRAFT CARRIER

WELL, AS LONG AS YOU'RE HERE, I MIGHT AS WELL CHECK YOU FOR ANY DEFICIENCIES

I DON'T WANT YOU TO BECOME ANEMIC

DON'T FORGET BERIBERI, RICKETS AND SCURVY, DOC

SOMETIMES PEOPLE WHO SUFFER FROM VITAMIN DEFICIENCIES AS A RESULT OF DIETING

... CAN BECOME LISTLESS

THEY CAN ALSO BE IRRITABLE

OR NERVOUS

SOMETIMES THEY SUFFER FROM AN UNCONTROLLABLE TWITCH

THEY MAY EVEN HAVE DIFFICULTY BREATHING

GASP!

YOU KNOW, GARFIELD, MAYBE THIS DIET HAS BEEN TOO HARD ON YOU

I'D RATHER SEE YOU FAT AND HEALTHY THAN LIKE THIS

MAYBE I COULD LET YOU SKIP THE DIET FOR RIGHT NOW AND START YOU WITH SOME MILD EXERCISE INSTEAD. WOULD YOU LIKE THAT?

NOW THE FIRST THANKSGIVING WAS IN 1621. THE PILGRIMS HAD A GOOD HARVEST, SO GOVERNOR BRADFORD DECLARED A THREE DAY FEAST. YOU SEE, THEY...

RRRRRRR

WHAT'S THAT?

SOUNDS LIKE THE DISHWASHER

SOOO, AHEM. THEY INVITED THEIR INDIAN FRIENDS TO JOIN THEM AND EVERYONE BROUGHT FOOD AND THERE WAS...

EVER HAD GRANDMA'S FAMOUS TURKEY CROQUETTES, GARFIELD? NOTHING FINER

GO, GRANDMA, GO

"THERE NOW, WE'LL JUST WHIP TOGETHER A LITTLE WHITE SAUCE"

"A DASH OF LEMON JUICE"

"A BIT OF PARSLEY"

"SOME GRATED ONION"

NOW, I'LL JUST SLIP QUIETLY OUT THE DOOR, GARFIELD

A
Garfield
Christmas

JIM DAVIS

GRANDPA WAS A PROUD MAN. A STRONG MAN. HE WAS A GOOD PROVIDER. WE NEVER HAD MUCH MONEY...

BUT, WE ALWAYS HAD PLENTY OF FOOD ON THE TABLE, AND HE ALWAYS MADE SOMETHING SPECIAL FOR ME AND EACH OF THE CHILDREN AT CHRISTMAS

MEN LIKE HIM DIDN'T FEEL LIKE THEY COULD SHOW MUCH AFFECTION OUTWARDLY TO THE CHILDREN...

BUT, ON CHRISTMAS IT WAS OKAY. HE ALWAYS PRETENDED NOT TO BE EXCITED ON CHRISTMAS MORNING, BUT HIS EYES GAVE HIM AWAY

I THINK IT WAS HIS FAVORITE DAY OF THE YEAR. SOMETIMES I WAKE UP IN THE NIGHT AND I CAN STILL FEEL HIS STRONG ARMS AROUND ME

THIS IS THE NIGHT I MISS HIM THE MOST

YOU BOYS HAVE A GOOD NIGHT'S SLEEP

SEE YOU IN THE MORNING

NIGHT, MOM   NIGHT, MOM

CLICK

WELL. THAT WAS A VERY NICE CHRISTMAS

IT'S NOT OVER YET

ONE MINUTE...

WHY THANK YOU, GARFIELD. WHAT'S THIS?

OH MY. OH MY

YULE LOVE GARFIELD ON DVD!

This Never-Before-Available DVD Features Three Hilarious Garfield Specials: *Garfield's Halloween Adventure, Garfield's Thanksgiving,* and *A Garfield Christmas Special.*

Available To Own October 12, 2004!